From the

Nurse, and Caregiver

A Daughter's Journey of Duty and Honor

Photo Credit: Diana L. Hughes

By Dr. Cynthia J. Lewis-Hickman

ISBN: 978-1-7337981-0-5

Printed by Reaching for the Mark of Excellence Publishing Company, in the United States of America.

Reaching for the Mark of Excellence Publishing Company

Email: cjhbeh@msn.com
https://cynthiajhickman.info/

Scriptures marked KJV are taken from the KING JAMES VERSION (KJV): KING JAMES VERSION, public domain.

Dr. Cynthia Lewis-Hickman

The role of caregiver lasted 20 years. Some good, some not so good, but still, I would not have changed a thing! Here is my anthem for that season of my life.

It Is Well With My Soul!

When peace, like a river, attendeth my way,

When sorrows like sea billows roll;

Whatever my lot, Thou hast taught me to say,

It is well, it is well with my soul.

Though Satan should buffet, though trials should come,

Let this blest assurance control,

That Christ hath regarded my helpless estate,

And hath shed His own blood for my soul.

My sin, oh the bliss of this glorious thought!

My sin, not in part but the whole,

Is nailed to His cross, and I bear it no more,

Praise the Lord, praise the Lord, O my soul!

For me, be it Christ, be it Christ hence to live:

If Jordan above me shall roll,

No pain shall be mine, for in death as in life

Thou wilt whisper Thy peace to my soul.

And Lord haste the day when the faith shall be sight,

The clouds be rolled back as a scroll;

The trump shall resound, and the Lord shall descend,

Even so, it is well with my soul.

(Refrain) It is well (it is well),

with my soul (with my soul),

It is well, it is well with my soul.[1]

Credit: Philip Bliss (1876)

---

[1] It Is Well with My Soul. (2005, November 15). Retrieved from https://en.wikipedia.org/wiki/It_Is_Well_with_My_Soul

Dedication

To my amazing husband, Bernis E. Hickman who was by my side the twenty years mommy was in our home. Thank you for your love and support. Thank you for seeing the necessity for mommy to relocate to Missouri City, Texas to live with us. Going down those basement steps at 1618 Fernwood to do laundry, light the pilot on the hot-water heater, and shoveling snow needed to change, and it did! I will forever be grateful for your sacrifice and service.

Acknowledgements

To my Heavenly Father, thank you for the years you allowed mommy to dwell with us. It was an honor and a pleasure to care for her as she cared for us in our beginning. It was the culmination of her new beginning, and while painful to witness, her transition occurred within the parameters of much love from her family and friends. Thank you, God! Why? Because love conquered all!

To my family, sisters, my children, grandchildren, nieces, nephews, extended family and friends, know whatever role you played in making mommy's life special, thank you.

To Izzy, mommy's hospice nurse, you are one of a kind. You met her coming and going. The smile on her face when she met you will forever be in my heart.

Preface

This is a love story. A story of a daughter's mission to give her all in the care of her mother. It acknowledges the honor and duty of a daughter; adding sunshine to the twilight years, filling her life with appreciation, abundant overflow, and gratitude. Relocating to a new city and state after living in one spot for over 50 years, could not have been an easy task. Mommy left behind the city where she taught for three decades in Toledo Public Schools System, the city where her husband died, the city where she raised her four daughters, and the city where she worshipped for half her life.

It is a journey through the caregiver's eyes. It shares exciting times, difficult decisions, frustrations, anger, illness, the hospice experience, and death and burial. I tell this story because it is mine. Within the walls of 1415, the challenges and blessings of being a caregiver are stated in the most respectful and occasionally emotional articulations of my existence. Lest, I not forget, my helpmate who lived through many moments of mommy's life and endured my rants occasionally like, "I can't do this anymore...and where are my sisters?" He deserves a gold star.

I wondered how it would all end. Now I know. Mommy died on August 20th, 2017, seven days after her 97th birthday. A week before, we gave her the biggest birthday party. The smile on her face seeing us all together said it all. I wonder now, did she know? Did she plan her departure? Seeing us together one more time might have been what she had been waiting for. That day, changed my world forever. But through it all, I learned valuable lessons taking care of mommy. Being the nurse was easy, being the daughter and caregiver was hard. When you read this book, you will see what I mean. Furthermore, I pray this book inspires you should you find yourself in a caregiving role to give it all you got! I also pray if you are reading this book as a healthcare practitioner, you take away from it the need for compassion, empathy, and a better understanding of the difficult demands of the caregiver role. The role commits you to the "laying on of healing hands." Many days and nights, I suffered in silence, in tears about my true feelings and emotions associated with this role called a caregiver. My attitude, behavior, response to others and emotions somehow created this wall or reasoning behind the lack of participation in mommy's care. There were many sleepless days and nights along the way. The social butterfly was no longer social. I was the chosen one. Born for such a time as this…the care of my mother. I retired from my employer, St. Luke's Episcopal Hospital in the Texas Medical Center on August 13th, 2013 to become a full-time caregiver. Does that date look familiar? After returning from a national conference, it became obvious the juggling of vocation, coursework, spousal duties while burning the midnight oil was beginning to affect my health. Something had to give! I told myself I can get another job, but God only gave me one mother. The need to be present as health challenges encapsulated our daily lives was my priority. The last five years of mommy's earthly journey required more and more attention as various health challenges weakened her body (not her spirit). The sacrifice was personal, anchored in honor and duty. In one of my low points this scripture gave me resolve for this journey:

*Whatever you do, work at it with all your heart, as working for the Lord, not for men…*Colossians 3:23

Scriptures will appear throughout this book. Mommy loved reading the bible and applying scriptures to life. For me, this constant reminder helped me complete this journey. Decisions made along the way were guided by the reassurance that God ordered and directed my steps. I've been told many times over; mommy's life was extended because I embraced the gift of caregiving; coupled with the art and science of nursing. Yes, I'm grateful for the strength and skills to endure, but what I would give for one more day with her…

I miss mommy… wondering if you miss me (rhetorical)?

Cynthia J. Lewis-Hickman

Table of Contents

What Went On Between the Dots!

1920….2017

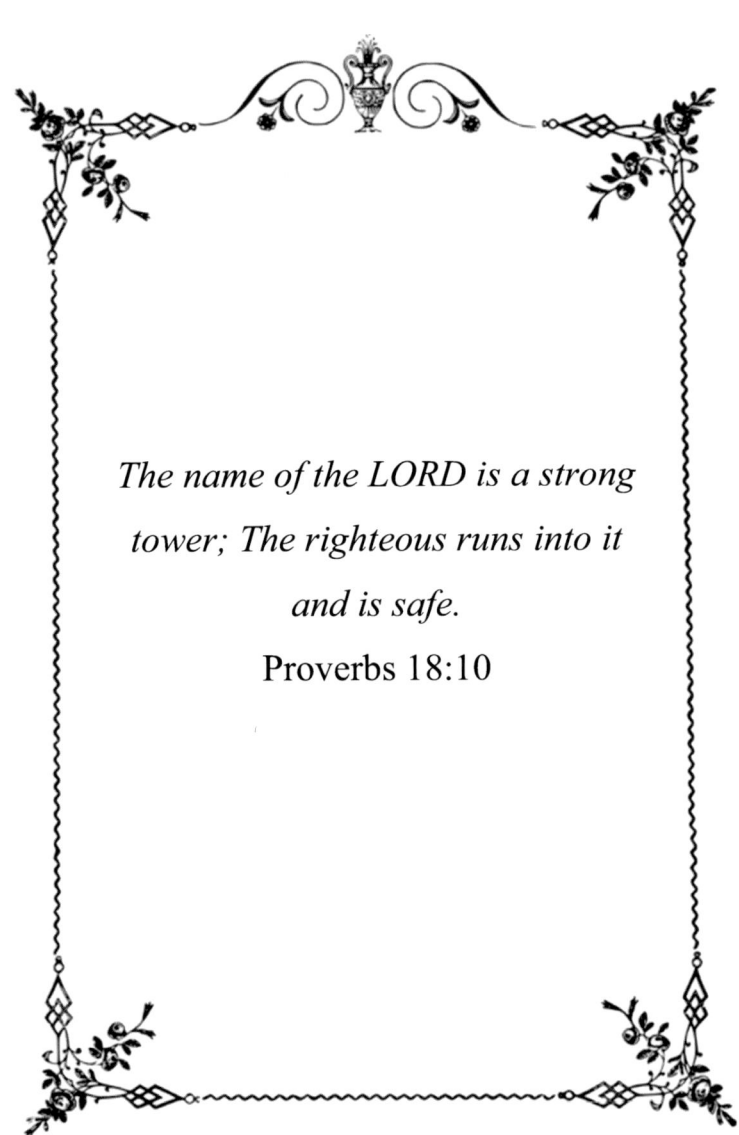

The name of the LORD is a strong tower; The righteous runs into it and is safe.

Proverbs 18:10

CHAPTER ONE

The Move

Nineteen ninety seven was a very good year. It was the year mommy moved to Missouri City, Texas to live with us. I am sure it had to be a difficult and bitter-sweet decision. She had lived in Toledo Ohio for over 50 years. My father, James C. Lewis, died on April 20, 1965. She became a widow raising four girls and embracing all our memories. She had property. She had relatives, a church family, loving neighbors, and many friends. She was employed by Toledo Public Schools (TPS) over 30 years. She taught science at many elementary and middle schools in Toledo school district for thirty years. Leaving the life she knew could not have been easy, but mommy realized the challenges associated with aging and living alone, she understood a change was imminent.

She made several visits to Texas before she took the final plunge. My sister, Diana Lynn had lived in Texas for many years and visited with her on occasion. Spending time in Texas, I'm sure, was helpful in the transition process. She also made annual visits to Toledo to hang out with my older sisters Anita and Brenda and that was helpful as well. My hubby and mommy made the drive from Toledo to Texas. Mommy drove part of the way (Oh, did I tell you, when mommy moved to Texas, she was still driving). She had purchased a 1993 Plymouth Acclaim. It was white with a red interior. Mommy had property in Ohio, but she eventually handed it over to my sisters.

One of the first conversations I remember having with mommy was that I was not interested in managing property 1,500 miles away. I told her its, "…just not my cup of tea." Over time she found that to be true as well. However, she had a request because she loved her family selflessly. She said, "please keep the property in the family. You never know when someone in the family may need a place to stay." I'm sure she repeated that statement to my sisters who were still living in Ohio. That was the spirit of my mommy. She was continually looking out for her family.

Mommy eventually settled in Texas. Our home became her home. I was excited to have my mommy with us. It took her a while to settle in and when she did, there was no stopping her. A lady at church invited her to visit a senior center not far from the house. After a few visits, she was hooked. Monday through Friday, she found her hangout. While at the hangout, she found something else. Can you say, man-friend?

Soon mommy was out and about with Mr. Henry, her newfound friend. Mommy was doing her thing (as the young folk would say). Then I noticed something. She was always driving wherever her, and Mr. Henry would hang out. So, being the observant daughter that I am inquired. "Mommy, why are you always doing all the driving?" Her reply, "When I am ready to go, I can get in my car and won't have to wait on nobody, and besides, Henry does not drive." Well, I guess she told me. I was finished with that conversation. Wisdom spoke, and her decision was unhindered. That was that!

Mommy enjoyed many happy times attending the senior center. When the manager found out she was a retired teacher, they put her to work. Mommy was a lifelong learner. She enjoyed teaching and sharing past, present, and current events with others. The manager of the center asked mommy if she would bring short stories on topics that highlighted annual holidays and history. She agreed, and soon newspaper articles and books started filling her space.

Her room begin to look like a classroom and the local library. The only thing missing was a blackboard, (You know that thing you write on with chalk). She was in her element. Writing her ideas on papers, the back of book covers, scratch paper. Wherever there was an empty space to jot a note or idea, she would do it. She kept tablets, notebook paper, and calendars. I even found a joker from a deck of cards with a note she kept about a black history soldier. She was a great writer, educator and researcher.

She would often ask me to research her topic and then print it, so she would be prepared when she spoke at the center. Sometimes I would say, *"Mommy, this is your ball a wax…why you are pulling me into your research party?"* She would say I was so good on the computer and it would not take me long to find what SHE needed. Of course, I delivered. What was I supposed to do… say no? (*Boy, do I miss those moments in time*).

Her wisdom was so unselfishly shared with others. She was a true educator. Mommy influenced so many people, and her family members were right in the mix. Every day we got a lesson, there was always a teachable moment, a shared quote from the bible, or a reminder of something that was just downright common sense. We were blessed to live in the circle of her influence. She trusted God, for as long as I can remember; but for sure, I experienced it firsthand, the twenty years she lived under our roof. The years were filled with fun, laughter, travel, instruction, connecting, reproof, sickness and health, fashion, nail polishing, and unconditional love.

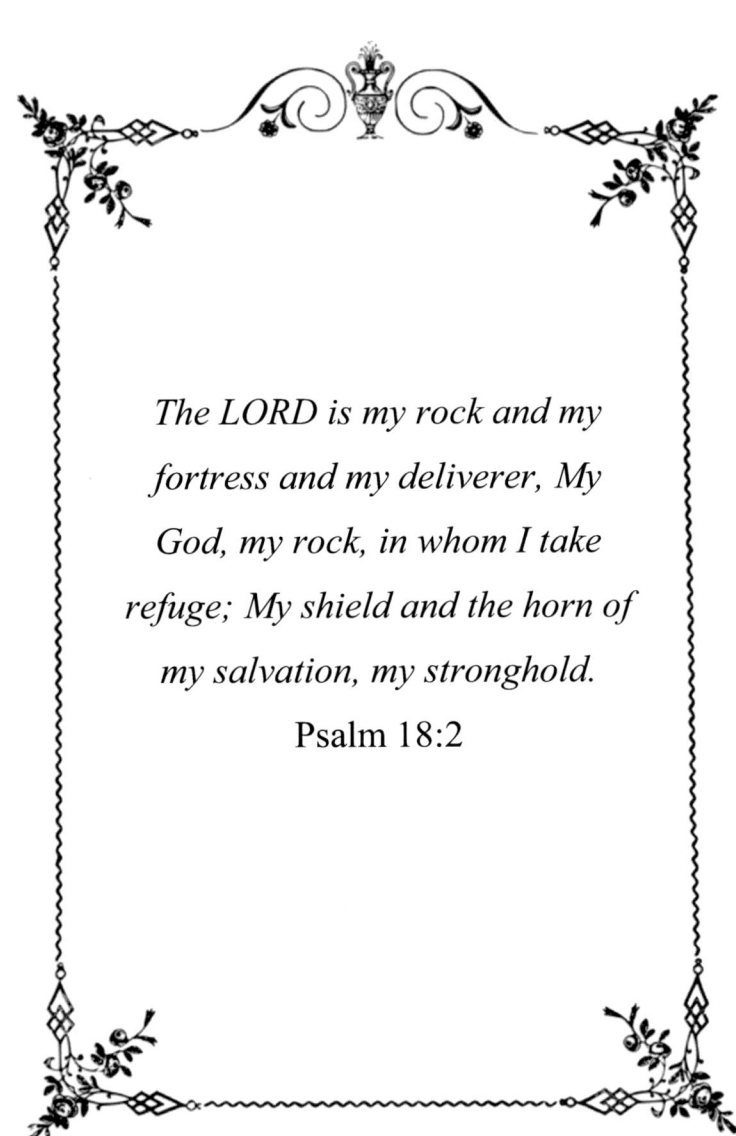

The LORD is my rock and my fortress and my deliverer, My God, my rock, in whom I take refuge; My shield and the horn of my salvation, my stronghold.

Psalm 18:2

CHAPTER TWO

Family and Travel

In mommy's earlier years in Texas, we did a lot of traveling. Hanging out with family was dear to her. Mommy celebrated birthdays, weddings, graduations, and funerals. Hubby and I made it happen. Just seeing her excitement and soft smile when around family was incredibly priceless. One of the most consistent characteristics about mommy was her commitment to family first, of course after God. She demonstrated her gratefulness to God by appreciating his daily blessings. She taught me to seek God in everything, often telling me. "He will give you peace…just trust Him." I can still hear mommy saying these words to me when I was distressed and feeling beat down, "Cynthia…Jesus loves you."

I remember one conversation we shared about being the last family member from her parents, Walter Wiley and Lillian Smith. It made her very sad. Her sister, Molly Smith died on February 5th, 1998. It shook her deeply. She said, "I'm alone now." Mommy was a strong woman, but this news showed her vulnerable side to family loss. Two-weeks prior, she had talked with Aunt Molly on the phone. I am grateful to have dialed that number.

When her sister died, we traveled to Hamilton, Ohio, Butler County. Hamilton was where mommy spent her formative years. She attended college at Wilberforce University, the only one of her siblings to attend college. Education, however, did not change her. She used it to benefit others. That was a strong suit for mommy. If you were in her midst, you participated in many teachable moments.

Since mommy and I did not have a lot of knowledge about Texas history we visited several famous landmarks like, “The Alamo,” “Battleship Texas,” and the “Black Buffalo Soldier of Texas Museum.” We went to Austin to visit the State Capital, and also to Houston’s Museum of National Science. At the Houston Museum, my sister, Diana and I took mommy to an array of interesting displays and interactive programs. I remember one cognitive interactive program that tested memory and eye-hand coordination. Mommy participated in the interactive program. I remember laughing so hard at her slow uncoordinated, but funny responses. But in my mind, I was seeing something much more concerning as the daughter/nurse/caregiver. We made it through the rib-tickling laughable exercise, but I had bigger concerns after watching mommy struggle with a few simple tasks. Her brain was working fine, but she could not see with clarity. She would remember the spot, but would almost put a peg in a hole, or when she got over a hole, she would slide it into the space, versus just placing the peg. I thought to myself, part of her vision was missing. She was wearing spectacles that did not seem to offer her provision. Further investigation, followed by eye examinations uncovered my suspicion… mommy had cataracts. "Small bump in the road mommy. We got this!" Many bumps in the health road were on the horizon. I wondered, if seeing them coming, could any preparation on my part have softened the blow? Another rhetorical question. Sigh!

The cataract surgeries went well. They were done six months apart. The worse eye was operated on first. Mommy commented that she did not know she was going blind. Removing just one cataract made a huge difference to her vision. While she was recovering, I noticed that she was reading without her glasses. I'd say, we hit a home run. Following the second cataract surgery, mommy's vision was 20-20. It was better than mine without cataracts...*what's with that!*

Cataracts form clouding of the clear lens of the eyes. I asked mommy had she realized the changes in her vision. She stated she had when she was reading the bible. The print was foggy and blurred. She also mentioned it was harder to see when we were out at night. She thought it was her glasses. I thought so as well, blaming it on the fact that it was time for her bi-annual optometrist visit.

Thinking back, the nurse and caregiver (*ME*) realized that she experienced many of the symptoms associated with cataracts way before she became symptomatic. Double vision should have been a red flag for me. I would watch mommy sometimes move a book or newspaper in various directions to bring focus to the document. She would keep her lights on because of the increased difficulty in focusing in dim lighting. Glaring occurred from time to time when she would read some material and at times, she was sensitive to light.

Assessing the needs of the person you are caring for is an art and a science. The key to any health challenge as a caregiver is addressing the problem when it is identified.

The peace of mind comes knowing her vision was restored and mommy was back up and running after all the eye drops and dark shades. I must admit, she sure looked cool in those shade's and they made a real fashion statement! Don't believe it!

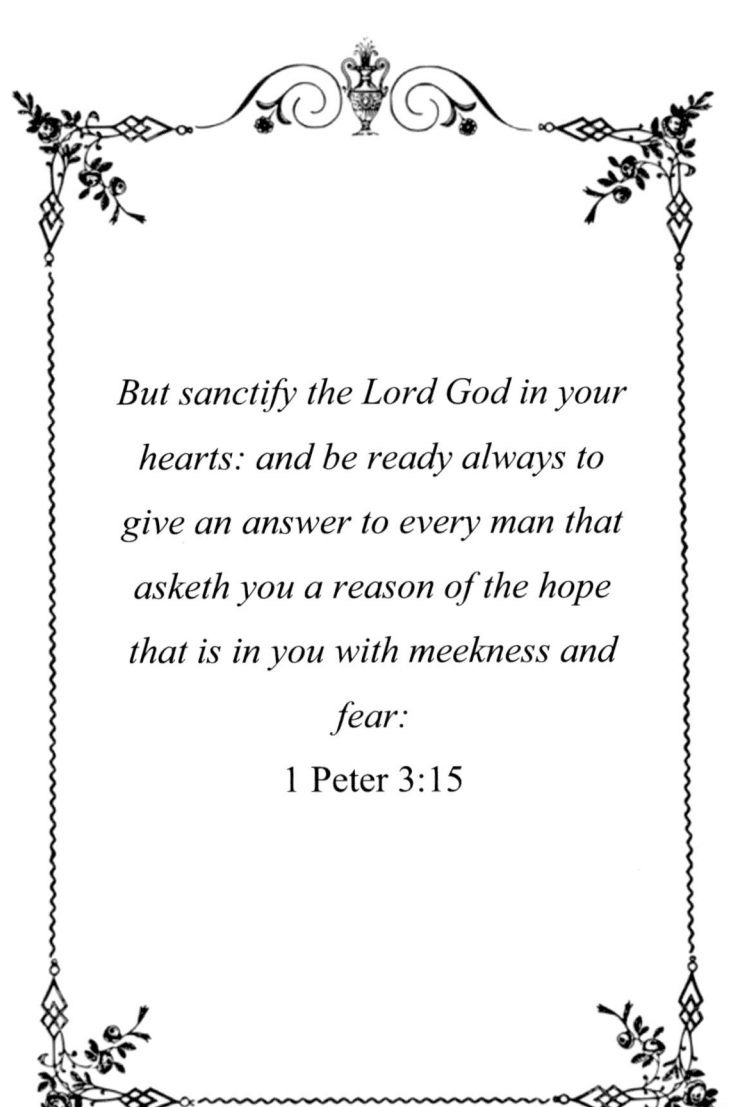

But sanctify the Lord God in your hearts: and be ready always to give an answer to every man that asketh you a reason of the hope that is in you with meekness and fear:

1 Peter 3:15

CHAPTER THREE

The Red Pen

When I determined it was time to leave my job, (*on August 13, 2013, sounds familiar*) to stay home with mom, I was in graduate school. Since mommy was a teacher, I thought to keep her brain sharp, she would spend her time proof-reading and editing my dissertation chapters. I remember, as if it was yesterday, mommy coming home from school and grading the papers of her pupils. Taking advantage of the red pen was my sly way of encouraging mommy to read to keep her 93-year old brain engaged. The goal was to help me pay attention to details; you know, comma placements, semi-colons, periods, hyphens and all that grammar stuff. And let's not forget the instructions on when to use; *bear* versus *bare, their* versus *there*, *whole* versus *hole*, and *til'* versus *until*...you get the picture. I had the best educator of all times at my disposal; living with me, in my space. She was always willing to instruct, encourage, chastise in love any paper I placed before here. Little did I know; my writing and grammar would be called into question by the matriarch of the family.

I recognized, when I invited mommy into my dissertation stratosphere, I was not prepared for the magnitude of her feedback with the red pencil. I figured a little red mark here and there. I presumed a few misspelled words would be called to my attention, or a run-on sentence that she found or an incomplete thought would be minor infractions. I knew if something was wrong or missing, or awkwardly worded, she would find it! Mommy always encouraged perfection from her girls. I was one of the girls and was not spared the judgement of the red pen.

When the red pen smoke cleared, I said to myself…I will never give mommy another document to read. I was tired of writing, editing, re-writing, more editing, changing sentence structure, adding sentences for clarity, and all that jazz. None the less, she did not have any mercy on her favorite daughter (*my sisters are going to kill me for this detail*). It has been said that a picture paints a thousand words. There is nothing else to say. I do wish I could give her another page to edit. My editor is on vacation … imagine that…without me.

The Red Pen

It is a method that addresses
erception of a phenomenon from
(Tuohy et al., 2013). It has been
ience having insight into the
uohy et al., 2013, p. 18). In this study,
E benefits obese AAW. There is equal
cial and cognitive explanations in the
preclude behavior aimed at healthier choice
nitive theory (SCT) will be considered when
ognitive construct of AAW. Self-efficacy, self-
n, and forethought are perspective tha
nding the human capability possible in deter
Bandura, 1986). This theory may be integral in the
porating improved nutritional food choices that could lead

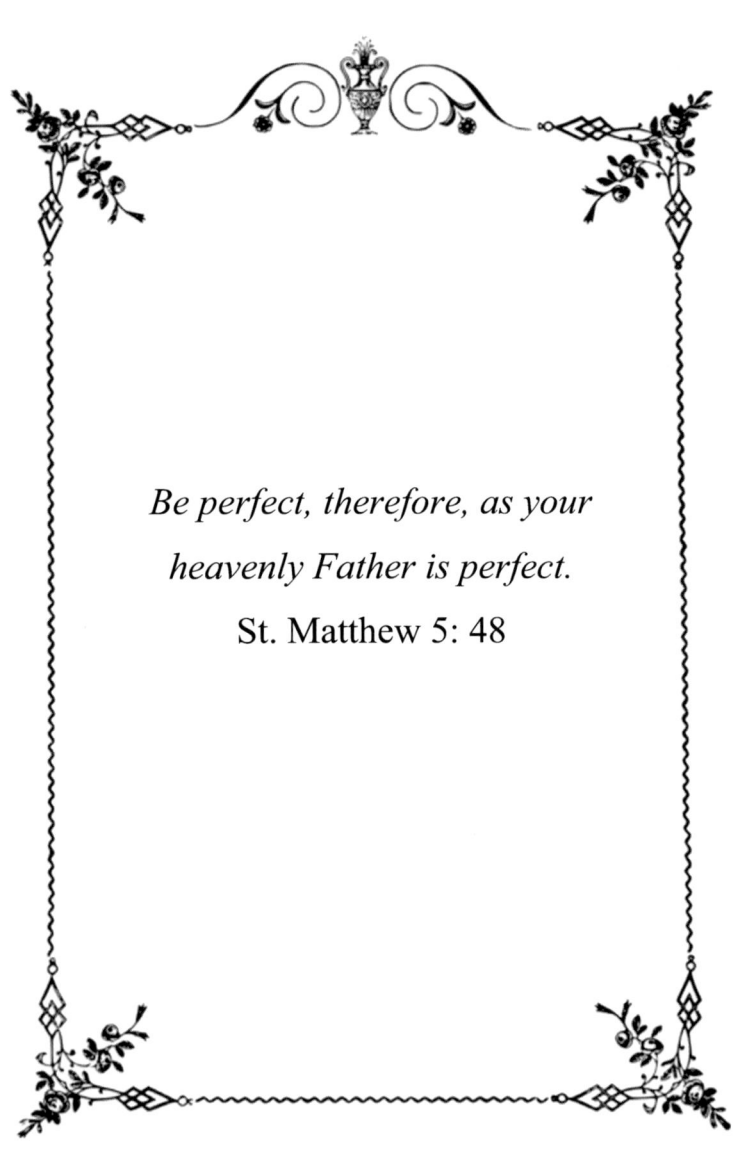

Be perfect, therefore, as your heavenly Father is perfect.

St. Matthew 5: 48

CHAPTER FOUR

When It All Changed

As the years progressed, mommy endured various health problems. The signs were even more fluent as she aged. We often look at life in the simple paradox of getting up every morning and going to bed every night. Yet life can be so much more complicated than the simplicity of our thoughts or the deterioration of one's body. The sign of a leak in the physical building; as the song goes… *there's a leak in this old building, one day I've got to move.*

Over mommy's 97 years, hospitalizations and medical events were minimum when you put it in perspective. Mommy's first medical intervention after moving to Texas was a pacemaker. After her device, she got more pep in her step! Watch out! Mommy was back on the move!

Years later, mommy's knees began to give her trouble. Pain standing, pain sitting, and lying in certain positions. She tried a single point walking cane, then a quad cane for steadiness, but the canes were short lived. This was the first-time mommy had to rely on any kind of durable medical equipment. Seeing her with a cane bothered me more than it bothered her, but she did not let these silver poll objects stop her from her daily senior center excursion. Tri-City Senior Center was her favorite hangout of all time (other than church) and silver sticks were not going to cramp her style or activities. Unfortunately, the quad cane was short lived. She lost her balance one day, and on the floor, she went. She said her knee gave out. The right one was worse than the left one, so she started favoring her left side. I knew it was time to visit the orthopedic practitioner for a conversation. After seeing her x-rays, I knew the old knees' days were numbered. Decision time was at hand and new knees were in her future.

Mommy got two new knees in 2001 and 2003 respectfully. She recovered from her knee surgeries but had to go back to using a cane. As she got older, using a walker for safety was necessary. Seeing mommy with a walker was another sign that her independence was turning into dependent care. Paying attention to her movements during the remainder of her life was high on my radar. The bi-lateral knee replacement was behind us. Thank God!

In 2006, I received a call from her doctor concerning a recent mammogram. The news was…Cancer…say it ain't so! Who gets breast cancer at 86 years old…mommy? Bilateral lesions were found and identified as invasive carcinoma. The good news in all of this was the lymph nodes were benign. Mommy underwent a mastectomy and radiation.

The radiation therapy was Monday through Friday for a total of six-weeks. We scheduled treatment mid-day to avoid the morning shenanigans. After the third week of radiation, mommy started complaining of severe weakness and indescribable tiredness. Little did I know, radiation had side effects as well. I initially thought, this was going to be a piece of cake. All mommy had to do was lay on a table and receive her treatment. Her doctors ordered a series of lab tests based on our discussion about mommy's symptoms. We discovered she had become anemic. Anemia is defined as a decrease in the number of red blood cells or the amount of hemoglobin in the blood.

Anemia is a common problem for patients undergoing radiation therapy and mommy fit the criteria. Anemia is when the hemoglobin levels fall below the normal values (hemoglobin = 12-14 g/dl). Mommy's level dropped to 9 g/dl and efforts to correct her anemia was handled by iron supplements during the completion of the radiation therapy treatments and six-months after therapy was completed. She recovered as expected and got right back on her horse. Mommy did not let much grass grow under her feet. If she was feeling well, she kept it moving.

Over the next 11 years, there were few hospitalizations, but her last hospitalization was one we will never forget. It was the beginning of the end. It was filled with all the events I promised mommy would never occur "I guess one should never say never!" It was, however God's design. He planned the whole turn of events. I did not see it then, but I saw it later. More about that in a later chapter.

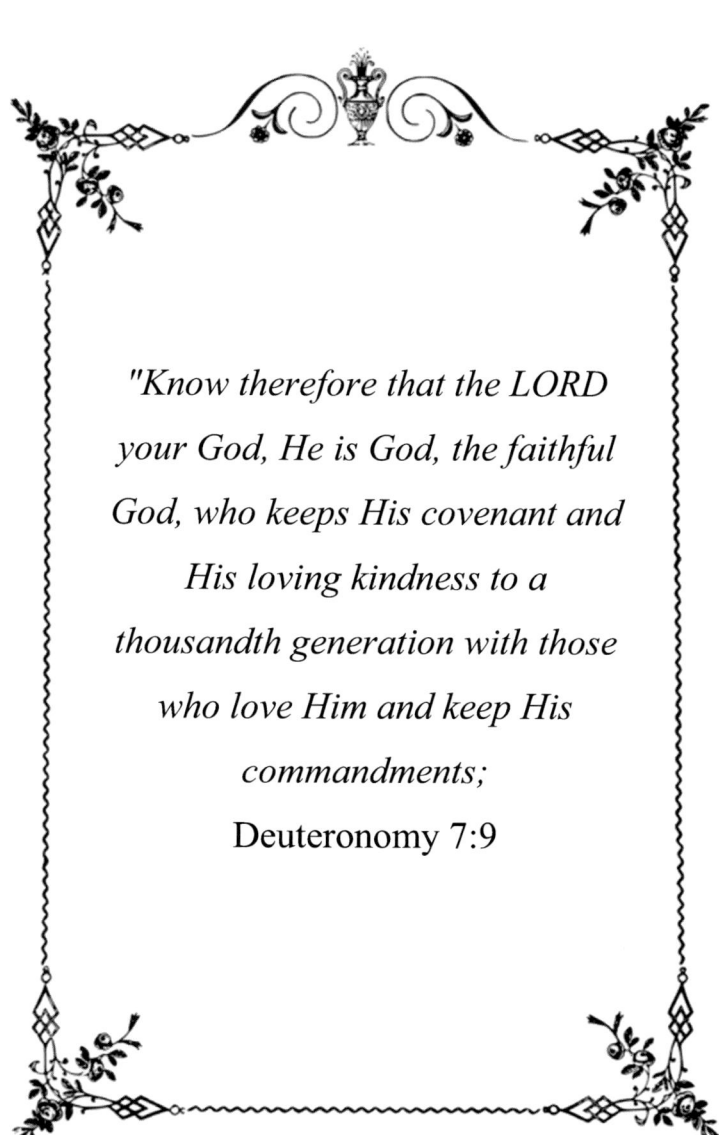

"Know therefore that the LORD your God, He is God, the faithful God, who keeps His covenant and His loving kindness to a thousandth generation with those who love Him and keep His commandments;

Deuteronomy 7:9

CHAPTER FIVE

Just Throw Me Away

It is 3 AM, and the bell is ringing. Ding, ding, ding. At 3 AM, I hated to hear that sound. It is a potty call. Five years ago, mommy used to walk to the bathroom from her room. She graduated to a bedside commode because her previous hospitalization made her pretty weak. She was admitted for acute renal failure. Her diuretics were doing their job, but they were also doing a job on her kidneys. She depended on hubby and me to help her out of bed and to the commode. We tried to put her on a schedule, but it did not work. So, we had to rely on her telling us.

Lord, what would I do without my help-mate? "Another rhetorical question." Some nights and days it was up, down, up, down, ding, ding, ding. Role reversal was in plain view. It was time to take into consideration the new norm. Mommy needed caring for and providing her needs, as she did for us growing up, without question, was my duty.

The realness of caregiving created overwhelming and unbelievable emotions. From feeling alone to "Lord why?" entered my thoughts many times. I felt a world of responsibility on my shoulders. Responsibilities surely others were much more equipped to take on. I was numb. I wanted out. I was completely questioning everything I knew or thought I knew. Even with my nursing background and experience, watching mommy decline and the role reversal in view, I was scared. My sisters would often say to me I was the best one for this job. What they really didn't know was, I felt they were best suited for the job. However, by this time, mommy had found great comfort and peace with my ability, so we forged onward… scared, fearful of the unknown, and wondering where this was going.

It was evident mommy relied on and trusted me. Accommodating her daily requirements became the new norm. It is called caregiving. I, along with my hubby, were her primary caregivers. We were responsible for meeting her needs. The role did not come with a time-table or end date. Caregiving addresses the 'whenever,' 'wherever,' and 'whatever' and any and everything in between.

Some days are better than others. Some days I would share how I was feeling (by ranting). Most days I suffered in silence. When someone asks what you need, I wonder if these people are blind. HELLO, folk I am caring for someone with a big smile and a heart that does not cook, clean, bathe on her own, do her laundry, polish her fingers or toes, comb her hair, or wipe her butt! No, it has not always been that way, but it is that way now! So, what is the question, again? What I wanted to hear was...what time did you say you were coming? Ten, eleven...that will be good. "I'll sleep in and you can sit up and respond to the bell." Most of my rants centered on being tired and sleep deprived. I forgot when the baby sleeps, you sleep. The reality… I was still working, going to school, participating in community projects, and nursing organization events. I was burning the candle at both ends.

My life was congested. My schedule was crazy. Enough about my schedule, caregiving was the new norm. And even with the new norm, my best did not feel worthy of the role. I remember apologizing many times for frowning, raising my voice, pouting, walking out of mommy's room, saying, "Where's my mommy?". Where was the lady that made the best tomato soup and grilled cheese sandwiches? Where was the mommy that would drive away and come home with bags of groceries, often carrying them in one hand? Mommy was so strong and quietly determined.

The real deal…I wanted my mommy back, but father time had its own agenda. While caring for her I wore the following titles of wife, mother, sister, aunt, grandmother, nurse, student, caregiver, caretaker, warden; custodian, guardian, overseer; administrator, boss, and steward. I wore each of them with honor ***(most of the time.)*** I tried to fill them all. I felt like a jack of many trades, but the master of none. Having a health care background and being armed with an arsenal of skills, still never prepares you for the last mile of the journey. I did my daily best in each of these roles; reminding myself that where God guides, He will also provide. I believe that is all that matters. ***Guess what? I never threw her away!***

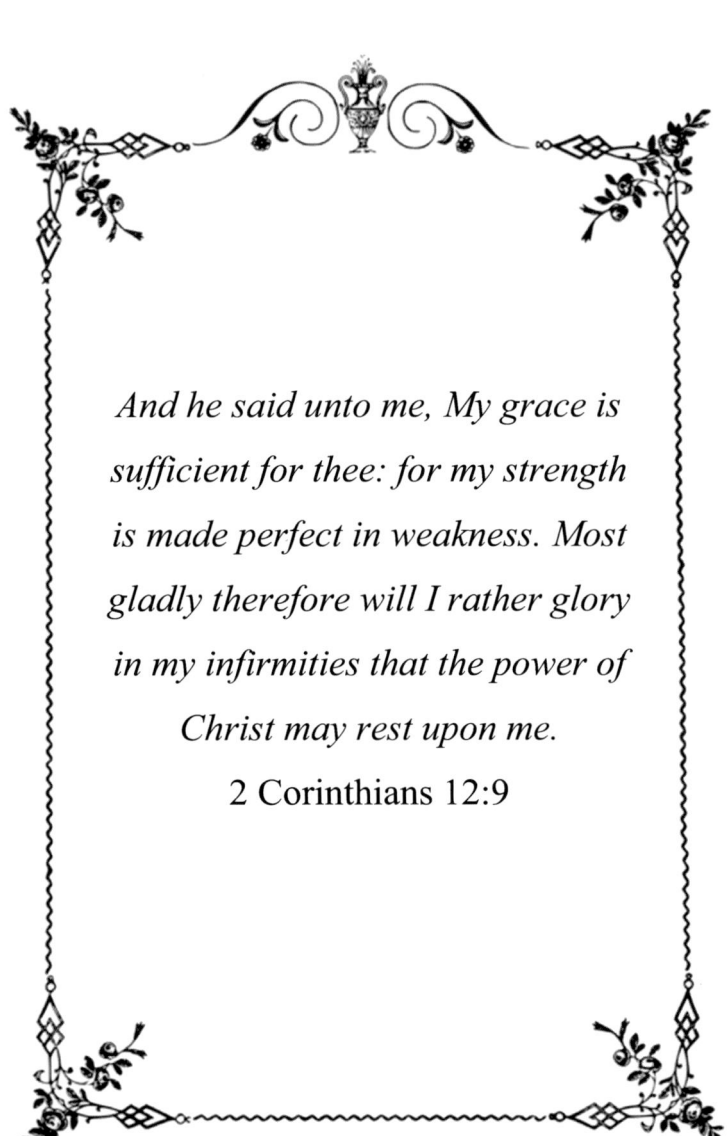

And he said unto me, My grace is sufficient for thee: for my strength is made perfect in weakness. Most gladly therefore will I rather glory in my infirmities that the power of Christ may rest upon me.

2 Corinthians 12:9

CHAPTER SIX

A Sign of What's to Come

The strangest occurrence one Friday morning troubled my spirit. Mommy called me in her room (ding, ding, ding …urrrrgh) and told me to sit down over there (over there was her brown comfortable lounge chair across from her bed. Oh no…not the green box content exploration). Do you think she wanted me comfortable as she prepared me for what was to come out of her mouth? She was still in the bed because the Senior Center was closed, so she had time on her hands. She said, "If I go before you, keep the family together." Where did that come from, I thought! I stared at her in wonder. "Um", was my first response, followed by a very long pause. "You want me to keep the family together?"

It was no secret mommy loved and adored her family. God was the center of mommy's life. She loved the song, *Child of the King*. Even with all our flaws, she saw nothing but good because she said…everything God made was good. Mommy wrote a lot about God, her life experiences and more. Here's an excerpt from one of her speeches.

Reverend and Mrs. Duane C. Tisdale

To: The Administrative Staff

To: The Platform Guest

To: Mrs. Pauline Harrison with special thanks for presenting me to you

To: All my sisters and brothers in Christ

There a sweet sweet spirit in this place.

And I know it is the Spirit of the Lord.

There are sweet expressions on each face

And I know it is the Spirit of the Lord.

When God says GO, the Holy Spirit will not only crown your head with wisdom and knowledge from on high, but it will lead, guide, and direct your path. In addition, according to Acts 1:8: "You shall receive power when the Holy Spirit comes, and you shall be my witness.

My friends, the Holy Spirit is here. The Holy spirit within us has a radiance that moves from heart to heart and from breast to breast when we are on one accord. The Holy spirit calls people, ordinary people like you and me through the Gospel and changes them from enemies of Christ into loving servants who demonstrate their faith by the way they live. Our theme this morning, "When God Says GO!"

Everyone needs a faith to live by. A self to live with, and a purpose to live for.

Let us pray:

Sweet Holy Spirit; Sweet Heavenly Dove; Stay right here with us; Filling us with your love; And for these blessings; We lift our hearts with praise; Without a doubt we'll know that we have been revived; When we shall leave this place.

John said, I was in the Spirit on the Lord's Day. Genesis 2:2 tells us God rested on the seventh day from all His work which He had done. The Sabbath was to be a day of recovery, as well as a day of sacrifice and worship.

My friends, today is Sunday. Today is your Sabbath; Today in this beautiful sanctuary let's lay aside every sin that so easily besets us. The Holy spirit has come and is prepared to anoint us this 1st Annual Missionary Day, September 30, 1990 with gifts and graces. Acknowledge the presence with Thanksgiving and accept your gift.

What is the gift for today? Some of us have had an opportunity to see some of God's magnificent awe-striking creations. One of the most outstanding is in Yellowstone National Park, west of Wyoming.

Old Faithful is not the largest geyser nor does it reach the highest height; never-the-less, it is by far the highest most popular geyser. Its popularity is due mainly to its dependability. You can count on old Faithful. Faithfulness is a great virtue.

Faithfulness is the hallmark of a spiritual leader. If you are present in this audience this morning, you are a spiritual leader.

You might say, "I haven't joined the church or I am not doing everything that is pleasing in the sight of God… Believe me you are not alone.

But my friends, when you woke up this morning, your mind was stayed on Jesus. Someone knew there was something different about you, your family, a neighbor or a friend. You have made a good impression on someone.

When God says GO—Go with faith, believing that all things are possible and that you can do things through Christ. This assurance is recorded in Philippians 4:13.

Before His ascension, Jesus gave His disciples a commission. Today we call it The Great Commission. He had previously given them a limited commission to go only to the Jews. His new commission was worldwide in its scope.

Jesus insisted that His disciples take the Gospel to others. Therefore, He instructed the apostles to GO. *"Go ye therefore and teach all nations, baptizing them in the name of the Father, and of the Son, and of the Holy Ghost; teaching them to observe all things whatsoever I have commanded you; and lo, I am with you always even unto the end of the world."* (Amen) Matthew 28:19 – 20

Christians are expected to teach or preach the good news of the death, burial, and resurrection of

Christ to all nations. The conditions of salvation are simple. A sinner must believe in Christ, repent and be baptized in the name of the Father, Son, and Holy Ghost.

When God says GO—Go teach men, women, boys, and girls how to live for Christ that they may receive the eternal reward at the end of the way.

Accept the gift of faith. Hebrews 11:6 tells us, *"...without faith it is impossible to please God for those who come to God must believe that He is a rewarder of those who diligently seek Him."*

Acts 2:17 reads, *"And it shall come to pass in the last days, says God, that I will pour out of my Spirit on all flesh, your young shall see visions, your old shall dream dreams..."*

Proverbs 29:18 tells us that, *"where there is no vision, the people perish."*

I looked at a program on television about an atomic energy plant. One section was being checked for radiation. It registered *danger zone* on the Geiger counter. One man said, "Man you are crazy to go up there." Maybe that is the attitude of our sinners, our bench members and our couch potatoes. Maybe they have more sense that we think they have. If they came up here, and God says to them, GO! They see a group of people that believe in miracles; a group of people that say, "I have to live with myself and so; I have to be fit for myself to know! I have to be able as the days go by to look at myself straight in the eye; A group of people that hunger and thirst after righteousness, and so they are drawn by this gigantic magnet to come to Sunday School and church and to come back Sunday afternoon if the church is open. All through the week they attend choir rehearsal, Bible Study, prayer meetings and missionary fellowships! This same group of power-filled people visit nursing homes, hospitals, and jails. They volunteer in shelters, schools, and community organizations such as First Call for Help, Metro-Toledo Churches United, Salvation Army, and the Church Women United Thrift Shop.

It's important that we know who we are, who made us, and who is in control. Psalm 100:3-4 states it simply and clearly, *"It is God who has made us, and not we ourselves; We are His people and the sheep of His pasture. Enter into His gates with thanksgiving and into His courts with praise. Be thankful to Him and bless His name."* Isaiah 43:10 reads, *"You are my witnesses and my servant whom I have chosen."* Galatians 4:6 – 7 tells us, "... *God has sent forth the Spirit of His Son into your hearts..., Therefore you are no longer a slave but a son and if a son, then an heir of God through Christ."*

Some of us are a little confused. We rely on Webster too much and not on the Holy Bible. We do not seem to know who is in control. Some of us act like wild animals. We forget that we are our Heavenly Father's children. We have been taught to pray *"Our Father Who Art in Heaven."* We are sons of God because we were created by God with the capacity to know Him and to choose to obey or disobey Him. He is the leader.

Accept your Gift of Faith. *...without faith it is impossible to please God [Him]*. (Hebrews 11:6)

May I repeat that everyone needs a faith to live by, a self to live with, and a purpose to live for; If you are a Christian, the Holy spirit will lead you to follow the gleam of God's dream for your life. You see God's dreams are so large that they require His help to make them come true. You remember the story recorded in Samuel 16:1, 12 – 13. *The Lord said to Samuel, "I am sending you to Jesse..., For I Have provided myself a king among his sons... and the Lord said "Arise, anoint him... Then Samuel took the horn of oil and anointed him... And the Spirit of the Lord came upon David from that day forward..."*

You *see* God matches His dream to the dreamer.

Have you ever wanted to change, but were afraid that someone would laugh at you or think you were crazy? Change is not always easy. Sometimes it takes a real jolt for us to change, like Saudi Arabia.[2]

In addition, once you accept Jesus as your personal Savior, many will not believe that you

[2] https://en.wikipedia.org/wiki/History_of_Saudi_Arabia

have changed. Your life as a Christian will not be easy. Hold to God's unchanging hand and yield not to temptation.

Everyone needs a purpose to live for, a cause to pursue, or a goal to be reached. One needs to find a need and fill it, a hurt and heal it, or a problem and solve it. This idea is not new. In Deuteronomy 15:11, we find these words, *"Therefore I command you saying, 'You shall open up your hand wide to your brother, to your poor and needy in your land.'"*

This is 1990! You are an "odd ball" if you do not have a cause. I have a cause! I am an advocate for Jesus Christ. I am a believer! I believe that Jesus is the answer.

In 1960 and beyond the popularity of the March blossoms.[3] Everyone carries a plague. I observed these unique bundles of humanity, these champions for whatever, and I came to the conclusion, that life could be so much simpler. We are suffering from

---

[3] http://www.lessonsite.com/archivepages/historyoftheworld/lesson31/protests60s.htm

complications. I cannot remember one march that was planned to show that God is in control.

The church gives you an opportunity to utilize your ability in fulfilling your desire to serve the Lord. I am an advocate for the family. I believe that Jesus is the answer to the disintegration of the family. No matter what definition you use for the family, people are looking for answers in all the wrong places. The family needs God. That's first. The Bible says, *"Seek ye first the kingdom of Heaven and its righteousness and all things will be added unto you."*

Unfortunately, we are like the Israelites. We are disobedient. We think we know it all. Deuteronomy 6:6-7 says, *"...these words, which I command thee this day, shall be in thine heart: And thou shalt teach them diligently unto thy children, and shalt talk of them when thou sittest in thine house, and when thou walkest by the way, and when thou liest down, and when thou risest up."*

In 1990, what do we have in our hearts? Has your communication broken down? In the book of

Matthew, Chapter 28, the word "GO" is used four times. The angel told Mary Madeline and the other Mary to go quickly and tell. Jesus met them and said go tell the brethren to go to Galilee. Eleven disciplines went into Galilee and met Jesus. He said go. If Jesus were here this morning in person, I think He would say go. Go believing that with God all things are possible…all things are possible. Go in peace and minister love in your home, in your community, and in the workplace. Go! When God says go, you will not go alone. For He said in Matthews 28:20, and *"…lo I am with you always, even until the ends of the world."* May God bless you always.

After reading mommy's speech did you connect the dots? She had a profound love for the family of God and her family as you will see in the next section.

Family Was Important to Mommy

She was always excited to hear from her daughters Anita Marie, Brenda Louise, Cynthia Jean, and Diana Lynn (the ABCD girls) and our offspring, what the families were up to, but most importantly she was more concerned with whether we stayed connected. Knowing how important family was to mommy, I told her I'd do my best. Under my breath, though, I was saying, nobody likes me. I was the angry, rude, tired, and sleep-deprived caregiver. I had demands, complaints, what's your problem issues, and family was either guilt-tripping or distant. Keep together…sure! Needless to say, the significance of the matter required me to dig deep within, mostly because I felt alone on this caregiving journey, but in reality, I love my family, and yes, they love me. I want to stay connected, even with all our flaws and imperfections. She said to me "I want you to know the family is grateful that you and Bernis are taking care of me." She even wrote about it. I found a note mommy wrote to me:

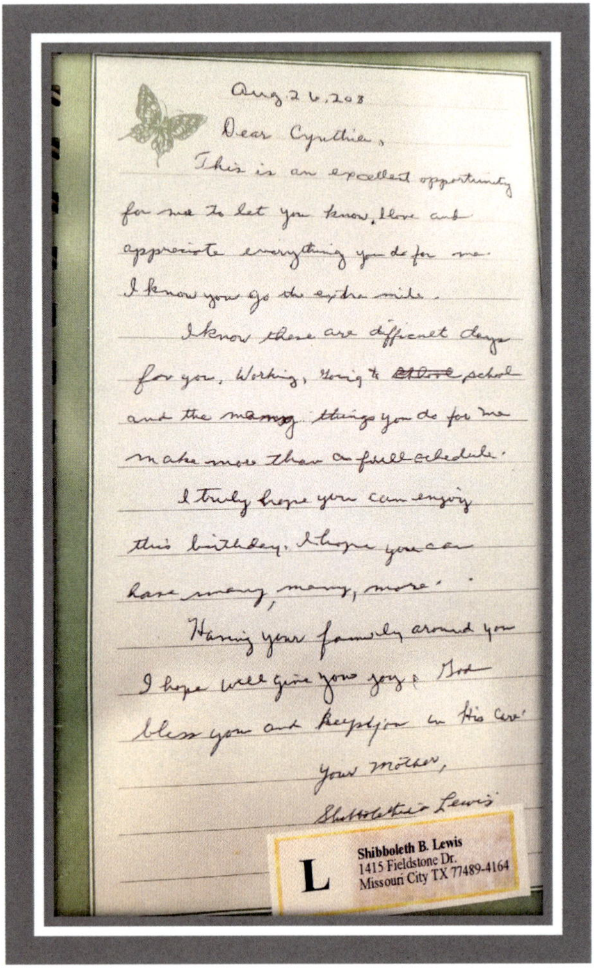

Aug 26, 203

Dear Cynthia,

This is an excellent opportunity for me to let you know, I love and appreciate everything you do for me. I know you go the extra mile.

I know there are difficult days for you, Working, Going to ~~[illegible]~~ school and the many things you do for me make more than a full schedule.

I truly hope you can enjoy this birthday. I hope you can have many, many, more.

Having your family around you I hope will give you joy. God bless you and keep you in His care.

Your mother,

Shibboleth Lewis

L
Shibboleth B. Lewis
1415 Fieldstone Dr.
Missouri City TX 77489-4164

Now back to the green box. Mommy asked me to get her green metal box from the closet. Every time we had a conversation about the green box, my anxiety level went from zero to one hundred. It's that feeling concerning the adage…they had that conversation with God and did not include you. Did mommy know something was coming? The green box held her important documents…insurance policies, birth certificates, and more. We had been over insurance policies with her so many times. However, this time was different. She had me call the insurance company and check on each policy. I had to make sure the dividends had paid the annual premiums, and all policies, specifically hers, was in good standing.

The lump in my throat as I went through that process stayed there all that day. I checked on mommy every 20 minutes that day. They ran over and over in my head, thoughts like… am I going to find mommy, unresponsive or even dead. Of course, we know, life is about death, but who wants to really embrace that concept. Not me! Clearly, this day I was mentally and emotionally a wreak. By the end of day, I was one exhausted caregiver. Need I tell you how the night went? I'm glad you asked! I stayed up all night. I told my husband I was pulling an 'all-nighter' doing school work. Honesty, I was checking the ABC's of life on mommy…airway, breathing, and circulation. Thank God Saturday arrived, and mommy was still here, and her smile always made the role of caregiving easier and worth it. "Thank you, Jesus, for one more day."

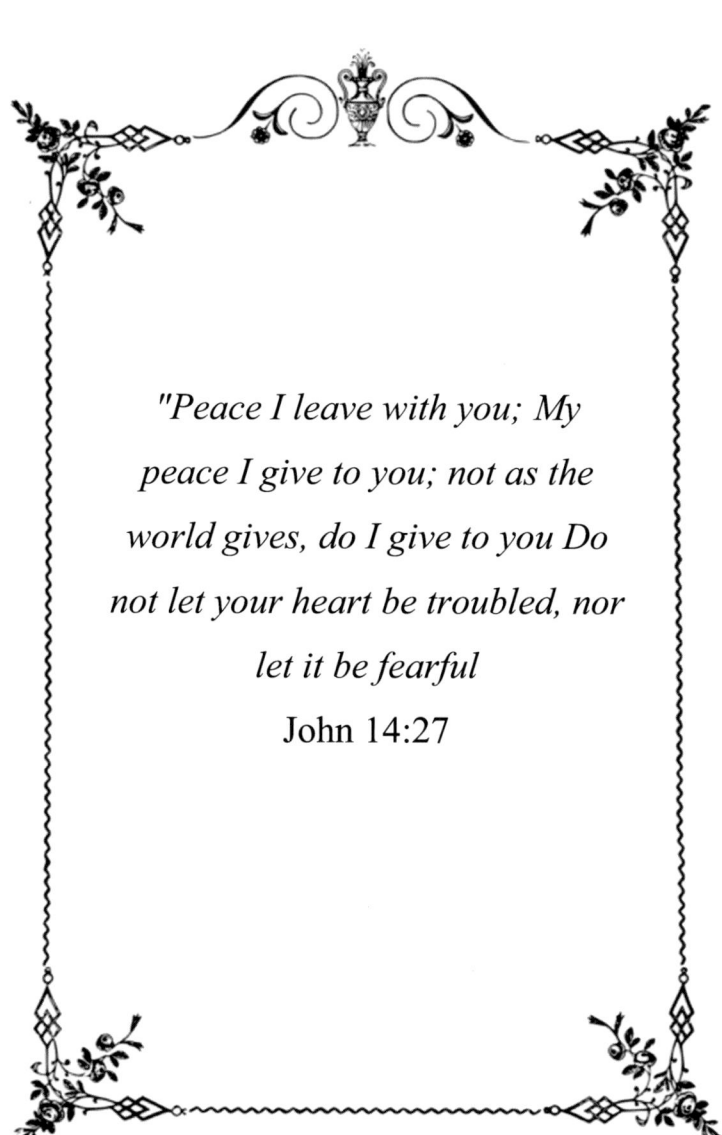

"Peace I leave with you; My peace I give to you; not as the world gives, do I give to you Do not let your heart be troubled, nor let it be fearful

John 14:27

Chapter Seven

Respite

There comes a time when everyone needs a break, especially if you are a long-term caregiver. In December 2016, I got word that my dear friend from my hometown was celebrating her 65th birthday and was planning a glorious birthday bash. I wanted to be there. We had been friends for over 35 years. Our children grew up together and she was my youngest daughter's Godmother and a huge part of my inner family.

I leaned on and consulted with my Texas family to work out a plan to care for mommy while I was away. I sent emails and made phone calls to ask for availability and suggestions to get 24-hour coverage to care for mommy in my absence. I realized my girls had families and jobs of their own, but in my self-centeredness, I did not necessarily care. My intent was directed toward the party in Toledo, Ohio.

While planning my trip, mommy along with my husband came down with bad colds and terrible coughs. How my plans for travel would work out came into question.

Did I need to dismiss my thoughts of a birthday bash with my friend? Wondering if a party was in my future, schedules began to surface of available dates and times my family could help care for mommy. After looking at the information, it became clear, I did not see that plan coming together.

Earlier in the year, my youngest daughter had suggested placing mommy in a facility that would provide respite care. I understood fully what respite care involved. I also knew about nursing home and skilled nursing facilities from my experience of being a nurse and healthcare advocate for over 25 years. Patients (some, not all) that were admitted to our hospital from nursing homes and skilled nursing facilities had preventable circumstances, decubitus (ulcers/bedsores). The development of these are the result of lying in one position for an extended period. Lack of personal hygiene, body odor from urine and feces and poor dental care. These are a few of my experiences caring for patients and it was not going to be something I would ever subject my mother to in a facility or anywhere else. I screamed... "OH NO, not my mommy!" My daughter worked for a Senior Care Corporation. She told to me it was different. She had observed how the staff and administrators worked to make their residents feel at home and they also do respite care. “Just try it mommy, please.”

I thought about it and slept on it for about a week or so. I finally agree to consider the thought. My daughter made the call for an appointment, so I could get the details of their program. This was a very arduous decision for me. Handing mommy over to strangers and the family not being vigilant was unheard of! Every hospitalization mommy ever had, we were there, 24-hrs around the clock. The thought of leaving her alone and my being out of town was anxiety producing to the 100th power. After touring the facility, speaking to different people, looking at where mommy would be staying, I conceded and agreed to place her in respite care while away.

Later that week, the admission’s nurse from respite care visited our home to complete paperwork and meet mommy. The entire visit I had tears in my eyes. All I could think about was the handing over of my mother to strangers, who did not know her or her needs; even though I explained them, wrote them down, reiterated them many times over. My anxiety and fear centered on communication, observations lost in translation, reports between shifts not being accurate, not attentive when she needed something and so much more. As I think about it now, these are all signs of a nurse working with multiple hospitalized patients and finding important things out after the fact which the reporting off nurse should have communicated during shift report. Anyway, I made it through the paperwork maze and signing my name 50 million times. I said goodbye to the representative wishing her a good day as she left with all my mother's personal and financial information.

My internal struggle continued. I went back to the emails from family to analyze and survey what I already knew. I was working hard to keep from putting mommy in this facility. When I looked at the schedules again, the family had shared and evaluating hubby's condition (remember, he was fighting a bad cold and cough) keeping mommy at home was not a good idea. My plan to keep mommy at home came down to abandoning my trip, staying home or checking my fears and anxieties at the door and making the move into respite care. I took a deep breath, cried some more, refocused and agreed to the respite plan, but decided to call it a retreat. Mommy was not senile. She still had her faculties. She knew the term respite care and she also had her own definition…throwing her away (of course, farthest from the truth). We made it crystal clear this visit was short term and my sister, Diana, the girls and their spouses would visit every day and evening while I was away. I saw mommy's look (you better not be lying staring over her glasses).

My focus, now changed to packing for mommy and packing for me. Packing for mommy was slow and steady. I let her pick what she wanted to take. We would also have conversations around all the activities available to her. Purposeful activities, ones that meet the needs of the residents and sometimes the community. Mommy was an educator and she enjoyed many fun and educational activities. We told her about French and Spanish class, physical exercise groups, cognitive exercises, eye and hand coordination groups, movie night and more. Another tip I shared was every day she would get up and get dressed and out of her room into a community setting to enjoy the other residents and pets that walked aimlessly about the grounds. I let her know she would be busy doing an array of activities to keep her engaged. Mommy bought into the retreat concept. The next question from mommy… "You will be back to get me, RIGHT? You are coming back?" With a stern face and demanding voice "YES" I'll be back!"

It was Wednesday on December 7, 2016, respite care move-in day. We had loads of items mommy would need while on her retreat. We had so much stuff two cars were utilized to transport all the things that would make her feel at home away from home. Needless to say, I again was an emotional wreck; emotional, teary-eyed, sick to my stomach, throat tight, and fighting with myself about whether I was making the right decision. So many mixed emotions, fears, concerns, worries, and down right scared. Willingly, I handed mommy over to strangers who promised to take good care of her, along with 100 other residents.

As we were met at the door of the facility, two attendants spoke to us and immediately took her clothes and other items to be labeled with her name. I had already done that before packing mommy's things, but they had their own system they followed, which means I wasted my time. I could have used that momentum to continue a justifiable rant (at least in my mind). The staffers stated they worked very hard to ensure the residents' personal belonging stay with the individual and if lost, they can be easily identified and returned to their owner. A noble and honorable concern. Thankful for their attentiveness to the personal belongings, but my concerns were far from stuff and things. I wanted insight into the 'who' 'what' 'where' and 'how' during mommy's stay.

As the staff settled mommy in, she asked to go to the bathroom. I immediately reminded them of my request of two people with mommy at all time. She had begun to have problems with movement and mobility and side-to-side assist was non-negotiable. One attendant headed to assist mommy and the look on my face said it all. "Who will be helping you?" "I can do it," she said." "We work with the residents all the time for bathroom needs." Wrong answer! "You don't know the needs of my mother, so I am telling you that another person needs to assist you." This interaction was not good for my psyche at all. They were meeting my mother for the first time. Taking care of familiar residents is one thing, but a new resident…it makes sense to listen to the family and that was the strongest point I could make. Now just so you know, an hour or so had passed and we still had not met the nurse on duty who would be admitting mommy, going over medications, answering any questions, so on and so forth. So, you tell me, how do you think I am feeling about now?

I had more questions than answers. If I was passing out grades, "D" would be the grade of the hour. It no secret, my emotions and anxieties were shining bright in full bloom. Every hypothetical negative outcome crossed my mine. The most debilitating and deepest anxiety centered on being 2000-miles away from her unavailable should I needed to get to mommy right away. Was I exhibiting daughter, mother, nurse, caregiver syndrome? Yes! It is real! Caregiver syndrome encompasses sadness, anger, anxiety, guilt, emotional confusion, perceived lack of trust, and despair, just to name a few.

The thoughts and feelings were crippling and exhausting. They had me shackled. I was emotionally unhinged about this respite care notion. Having a healthcare background did not help. In reality, all my actions and reactions had everything to do with my quest for excellence in the care of my mother. It had nothing to do with the facility, staff or nurses. The facility came highly recommended because my daughter had worked there and personally witnessed the staff in action. Many times, I was reminded by my daughter, that mommy was her grandmother. She said, "I would not put granny lady (that's what mommy was often called) in harm's way." This was the beginning of the personal storm calming down within my inside imprisonment. Not that I did not know the reality of role reversals, it was crystal clear I was the mother of my mother. The roles had internally and externally changed. The shift from daughter to parent was realer than it had ever been. This reinforced my duty to my mother and solidified a sense of honor to carry out this responsibility. My existence centered totally around the best care I could provide for mommy. Isn't that the provision of a mother's love? Unvarying and endless determination toward devoted and dedicated care.

As I relinquished my role as caregiving to the staff at the respite facility (I mean...*THE RETREAT*... remember I told mommy she was on a retreat), I returned home to complete the final phase of packing for my trip to Toledo Ohio. As much as I was looking forward to shaking a tail-feather celebrating my friends' birthday, every sweater folder and pair of socks bundled was an effort; thinking about what I was about to leave behind…my mommy.

December 7th was my travel day. I woke up emotional, drove to the airport emotional, flew to Toledo emotional and landed even more emotional. What is the first thing I did once my feet were planted on the ground? Yes, I did…called the facility to check in on mommy. I was told mommy was in a French class learning the language. After the call, the administrator sent me a picture of mommy. She was dressed, smiling, and sitting among other residents. This was the beginning of my emotional retreat. I turned my attention to why I was 2,000 miles away from mommy. The party would be happening in three days, so I gave up my emotional roller coaster, casting my cares on God and family so I could enjoy and celebrate my friend's great milestone. I deliberately transformed my thoughts and the corresponding action happened. I could relax and enjoy my time away. I realized; I was in respite mode in my birthplace and it felt wonderful!

Toledo, Ohio is my hometown, and I still had family there. The trip became a time to spend with my sisters, nieces and nephews and friends. Visiting with family and friends who I'd not seen for years was fun. As with any family gathering, talking about the good-old-days always makes you appreciate where you are in life. Learning so many of my classmates who attended Jesup W. Scott High School (*Go Bulldogs*) with me had died, made me pause and truly appreciate celebrating my friend. We danced, ate, laughed, took lots of pictures and shared stores of our children. My friend was my last daughter's god mother and when roasting and toasting, we realized we had a thirty-five-year relationship. *Oh my!* A great time was had by all. I am so thankful to have been a part of her birthday milestone. I am also thankful for my respite away from mommy. The time away from the caregiving role, rejuvenated me. But it also made me appreciate the realism of duty and honor. I realized that my duty did not end, by me removing myself from the caregiving equation for a time. I did not need to feel guilty about taking time away from it all. I needed to exhale. And exhale is what I did! It was good to change my geographic location for a time. The seven-day trip was tremendous. Taking a vacation built my strength and recharged me. Getting away revitalized me. Yes but, I must admit, returning home to mommy was the true highlight of the entire experience.

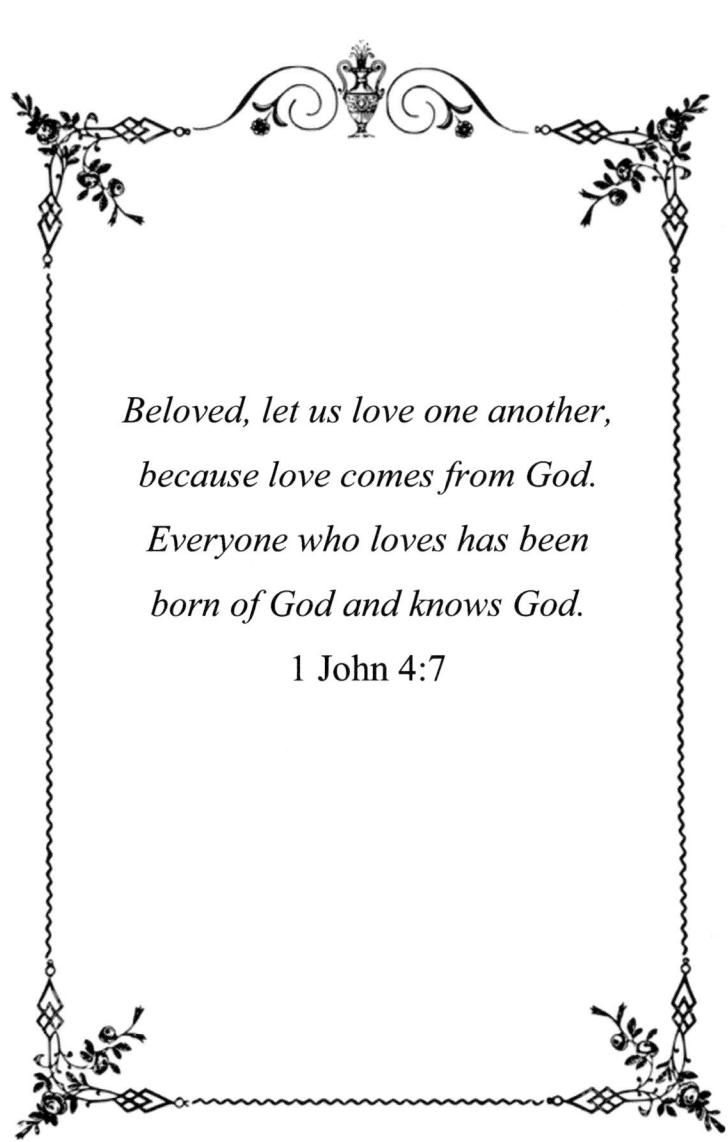

Beloved, let us love one another,

because love comes from God.

Everyone who loves has been

born of God and knows God.

1 John 4:7

Photo by Diana L. Hughes

CHAPTER EIGHT

Hospice, Heaven, Homegoing

The year of 2017 was a very sad time. I often wondered when and how it would end. What it would look like. How would I respond? How would I behave? What would I do? What would I say, or not say? Scream, yell, fall out, cuss God or stare in astonishment seeing mommy being positioned lifeless, breathless, motionless, still, tranquil, and peaceful.

It was early Sunday morning; seven days after mommy's 97th birthday, it happened. Mommy closed her eyes for the last time on earth. My sister, Diana and I were in the next room. The close vigil was because mommy hated the oxygen equipment. She would take it off every chance she got. She hated that venti-mask. She hated the nasal cannula. She could not stand the nebulizer treatments I administered every 4 to 6 hours. Mommy had a certain look when stuff was on and around her face. My sister, Diana and I were the respiratory police. The oxygen saturation monitor was a guide to make sure her saturations were at the proper levels. If mommy's saturation stayed between 96 % and 100% we were good.

Several occasions they would drop between 84% - 86% and she would become symptomatic. That is why we were the respiratory police between our short naps.

But early Sunday morning, August 20th, 2017 was different. Diana and I overslept. Caregiving can and does take a toll on the human body (I know now, God kept us asleep, to do his handy work). God knew we were sleep deprived and downright tired. He also knew mommy was tired. The last check was around 0430. While we were trying to get a few winks, Diana got up to check on mommy around 0530. I heard this loud, panic-filled shout… "Cynthia, mommy took off her oxygen." I jumped up to address the oxygen issue. I ran to the concentrator to turn up the oxygen and replace the nasal cannula with the venti-mask. While running toward the concentrator, I glanced at mommy and stopped in my tracks. She was quiet, warm, motionless, holding her teddy-bear in hand and gone. She looked so calm, relieved, rested, restored, everything we weren't. The journey ended. God had paid a visit to His earthly rose garden while we slept. He plucked His rose and she was gone, *Our mommy!* Our Queen!

I remember saying to sister, "Diana, mommy is gone … take mommy's hand, sit here by the bed. I need to make some phone calls." The first phone call was to the hospice nurse on call, Izzy. The blessing with Izzy is he admitted mommy into home hospice when she was discharged from the hospital on July 25th, 2017. He was the nurse that finalized the processes prior to mommy's transition to the funeral home on August 20th, 2017.

Preparing for mommy's homegoing service came together with the assistance of my siblings, children, grandchildren, and many supportive extended family and friends. My sisters have an array of talents. *Brenda Louise*, the eldest is our historian. She had a lot of knowledge of events that occurred over mommy's life. *Anita Marie*, second oldest, used her journalism major to write the obituary, newspaper, and journal announcements. The gift she has to bring words to life on paper was invaluable. Mommy's Obituaries were placed in the Toledo Blade, Toledo Journal, Sojourner Truth, Wilberforce University Alumni News, Church Women's United Newsletter, Missouri City News, and Houston Chronicle. *Diana Lynn*, the youngest is our creative sister. She prepared our attire. We wore blue to match *Our Queen.* Mommy was decked out, so we had to "bring it." As for me, *Cynthia Jean*, I handled the business and financial component of mommy's passing. Going through important documents and honoring mommy's request was my primary focus.

Mommy and I had many conversations about what to do and how to proceed after her passing. Her daughters were her #1 priority! Mommy loved her girls. She would often remind me of the importance of sisterhood. She would say, *"Love each other and look out for each other. Don't let distance keep that from happening and always make a great day. What do you do when you spill milk? Clean it up and keep going."*

Mommy went to heaven. I am still pinching myself. Knowing life is about death, you still never get ready for it. And you sure don't get ready for it when it is your mommy. How do you say goodbye to the one who knows you better than any earthly being? It is a rhetorical question. What remains are memories and a headstone. It is located in Houston Memorial Cemetery, Houston, Texas, Section Q 119. Her stone sits on a hill, easily located because of "that" name… 'Shibbolethia' cannot be hidden. Visiting a cemetery is not something I pictured myself doing. But I do. I take artificial flowers because they last longer. Why do I even bother? I think it's for me. Mommy is not interested in flowers. She is walking on streets of gold, not confined to her bed or wheelchair, no longer weary, and no longer unable to communicate.

I do have to admit that I wonder if mommy misses me. I ask that question more than you will ever know. I wonder if she holds me accountable for leaving her among strangers and alone, something I rarely ever did. Then it hits me, she is not alone. She is with the Father, my daddy, her parents, sisters, brothers, and friends.

Photo Credit: 3P EMAGES by Eric Lewis

So as the song goes…*Let the church say amen.*

God has spoken, so let the church say AMEN,

Our Queen… forever in my heart.

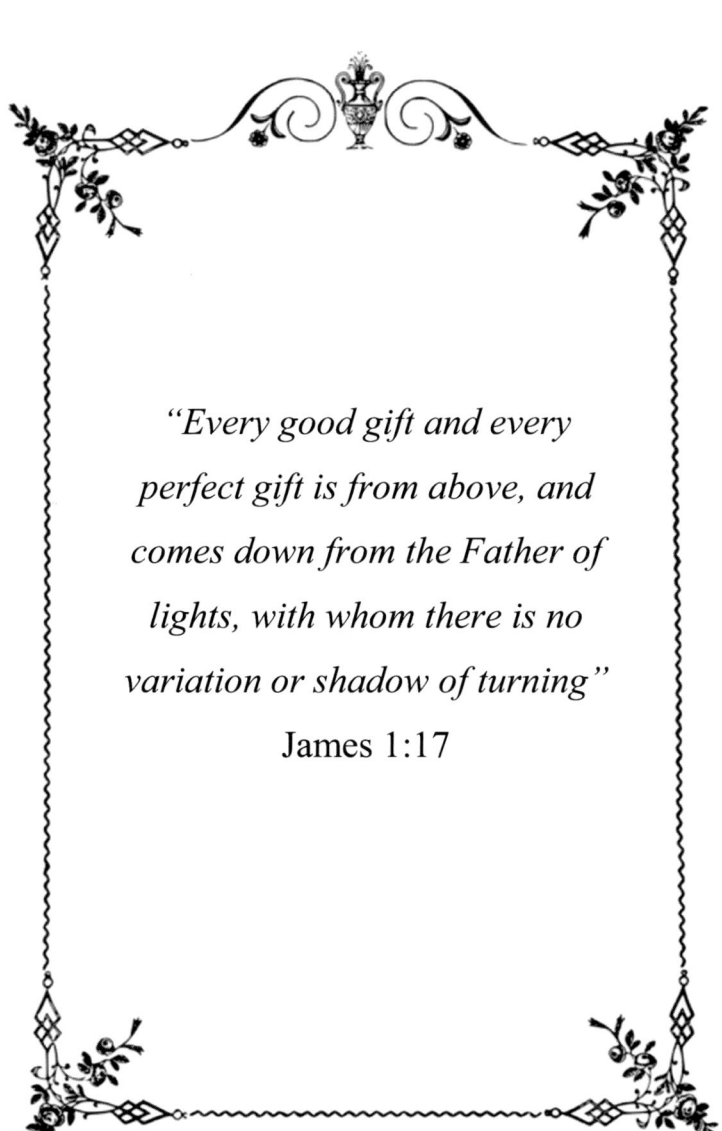

"Every good gift and every perfect gift is from above, and comes down from the Father of lights, with whom there is no variation or shadow of turning"

James 1:17

CHAPTER NINE

The Obituary

Shibbolethia.

The name, as unique, remarkable and lovely as the lady herself, came from the Hebrew Biblical word "SHIBBOLETH" found in the Book of Judges 12:6.

Shibbolethia Bryant {Smith} Lewis was born on August 13, 1920, in Shelbyville, Kentucky, the month and year that women were granted the right to vote.

Her father, Wiley Walter Smith, was a circuit minister for the African Methodist Episcopal (A.M.E.) Church, which required the family to move quite often when she was a young girl. Her mother, Lillian (Hoskins) Smith, was a homemaker who often worked as a domestic to help support her family. The family eventually settled in Hamilton, OH, where Shibbolethia (aka "Shibby") grew up with her sisters, Margaret and Mollie, and brothers, Emanuel and Paul. Several other children born to the family would die in their early childhoods.

Her maternal grandfather, Emanuel (Hairston) Hoskins, ran away from slavery as a boy. Mrs. Lewis often recalled that he operated a general store and a farm where he raised chickens and pigs. Her maternal grandmother's name was Maggie (Morris) Hoskins.

She attended Phillips Chapel (now St. Phillips Temple C.M.E. Church) and the public schools in Hamilton, graduating from Hamilton High School in 1938. Accepted to Wilberforce University and graduating in 1942, she became the first member of her family to attend college. She majored in home economics as academic options were limited for Black women.

Shibbolethia met her husband, James Clark Lewis, to a United Service Organizations (U.S.O.) event while she was in college. He was in the Army. While deployed, he sent his proposal of marriage by mail along with an engagement ring. This tiny five-foot-tall, strong-willed, feisty young woman refused to put the ring on her finger until James returned from his tour of duty to propose in person. She was 23 years old and he was 24 when they married on March 13th, 1944, in the home of her in-laws.

After her husband was honorably discharged from the Army, the couple lived in Florida and Youngstown before settling in Toledo, OH. Mrs. Lewis held a civil service job in Rossford, OH, while her husband worked as a mail carrier, and later as a cab driver. Four daughters were born of this union: Anita, Brenda, Cynthia, and Diana.

In the late 1950's, when the Civil Rights Movement opened doors of opportunity for African Americans, Mrs. Lewis returned to college to obtain teaching credentials, and started her professional teaching career with the Toledo Public Schools (TPS).

She earned her master's degree in Education from the University of Toledo in 1962 while working and caring for her family. As a grade school teacher, she taught a broad range of subjects - English, reading mathematics, and even music - subsequently impacting the lives of generations of students and her own daughters as well.

Endowed with a special interest in science, this gifted and innovative educator regularly involved her students in local and state science fairs where they were frequent award recipients. She introduced her students to museums and mussels; art and parks; stalactites and stalagmites, trilobites and constellations; aquariums, planetariums, volcanoes, and so much more.

A highly respected educator, she taught for many years at the former Roosevelt Elementary, then later at Gunkel and Jones Junior High Schools in Toledo. Mrs. Lewis is remembered to this day by many of her peers and students as a caring, creative, and skillful teacher.

Retiring after 30 years, Mrs. Lewis continued to make contributions in the areas of education, instructing adult literacy classes, and working periodically as a substitute teacher. Over time, many people and her neighbors on Fernwood simply knew or respectfully referred to her as the "schoolteacher."

Widowed in 1965, she became a single parent when her husband died from a heart attack. During this difficult time of her life, she had to assume new responsibilities that included learning how to drive for the first time.

A long-time member of the Phillips Temple C.M.E. Church in Toledo, OH, she served as Superintendent of Christian Education, conference delegate, missionary president, Sunday school teacher, and as chairperson for many programs, including Vacation Bible School. She regularly gathered carloads of children from her neighborhood and took them to Sunday school.

She was a kind and loving encourager who remained active in her church and community. Sayings she was known to share in response to difficulties and apparent failures in life were these: "What do you do with spilled milk? Clean it up of course;" If at first you don't succeed, try, and try again! Make a Good Day," and "I love you today!"

A prolific writer, she wrote articles for The Christian Index (a C.M.E. Church publication), poems, and narrative speeches. She published a collection of intercessory prayers in 1998. She is known for her "ministry" of calling, writing, and sending cards to encourage and to keep in touch with family and friends.

She was president of Church Women United for two years, and active in Toledo's City-Wide Missionary Fellowship. She was also a member of the Zeta Phi Beta Sorority, and a lifetime member of the American Federation of Retired Teachers.

Mrs. Lewis moved to Missouri City, TX, in August 1997, to live with daughter, Cynthia, and son-in-law,

Bernis Hickman, both formerly of Toledo. They welcomed her and served as loving and devoted caregivers for 20 years, providing her with a rich, full life.

Her favorite color was blue. She enjoyed the "Family Feud," and watching basketball, tennis, and Tiger Woods playing golf on television. She liked court TV with Judge Judy, Judge Joe Brown, and Judge Mathis. She also enjoyed crocheting and attending the Fort Bend Tri-City Senior Center with special friends. She was a wonderful cook, and she loved watermelon!

On October 13th, 2007, she was able to attend and celebrate her 69th high school reunion in Hamilton with the class of 1938. She was 87 years old at the time.

In November of 2008, at the age of 88, she was so happy and proud to cast her vote for the First African American President of the United States, Barack Hussein Obama; who sent her a proclamation in August 2010 acknowledging her 90th birthday.

Mrs. Lewis was faithful member and church mother at the Willowridge Baptist Church of Missouri City, TX, for many years prior to declining health.

Despite many life challenges, she remained a woman of grace, strength, character and perseverance, with a twinkle in her eyes and heart full of love for God and her family.

Mrs. Lewis, 97, passed away at her home on Sunday, August 20, 2017 under the care of Compassus Hospice - Houston. She was a resident of Missouri City, TX at the time of her passing.

She was preceded in death by: her husband, James Clark Lewis; great-grandparents, Richard and Hannah (French) Morris; grandparents, Emanuel and Maggie (Morris) Hoskins; parents, Rev. Wiley W. and Lillian(Hoskins) Smith; her siblings: Mollie, Paul, and Emanuel Smith; and Margaret Smith - Doyle; one aunt, Pearlena (aka 'Vanilla') Hoskins; uncles, Pete (Rosa Lee), and James (Minnie) Hoskins; a beloved niece, Margaret Wood; nephews, David Smith, Emanuel Merritt , and Kevin Smith; great nephew, Donald Wood; and great grandson, Feniks James Hughes.

She is survived by daughters: Brenda L. Lewis, RN, MSN-Ed; Dr. Anita M. Lewis-Sewell, BA, MD; Dr. Cynthia J. Hickman, RN, MSN-Ed, PhD; and Diana L. Hughes B.S.Ed., M.Ed.; Son-in Law, Bernis Hickman, a retired U.S.

Postal Service employee; grandchildren: Teresa (Zac) Hinton, Brenda (Donzell) Gulley-Moore, Bridgette Lynn Johnson-Ellis, Kerri K. King, Maria (Larry) Wilson, Michael (TerriLynn) Lemons, Ebrandia (Tyrone) Perry, James C. Hughes III, Jason T. Hamilton; nephews, Richard "Dick" (Jackie) Smith, Stanley Merritt, Timothy Fields, Henry Fields; special friend, Henry Farley, and a host of nieces, nephews, cousins, and great grandchildren. She was greatly loved and will be greatly missed by us all.

A Memorial Service celebrating the life of Mrs. Shibbolethia B. Lewis was held on Saturday, September 9, 2017 at the Warren African American Episcopal (A.M.E.) Church, 915 Collingwood Blvd. in Toledo, OH.

The Homegoing celebration for Mrs. Lewis was held on Saturday, September 16th at Willowridge Missionary Baptist Church, 2803 Staffordshire Road in Stafford, Texas where she was a beloved church mother.

The private interment service will be at Houston National Cemetery, 10410 Veterans Memorial Dr., in Houston, TX 77038.

Written by daughters of Mrs. Lewis:
Brenda L. Lewis & Dr. Anita M. Lewis-Sewell

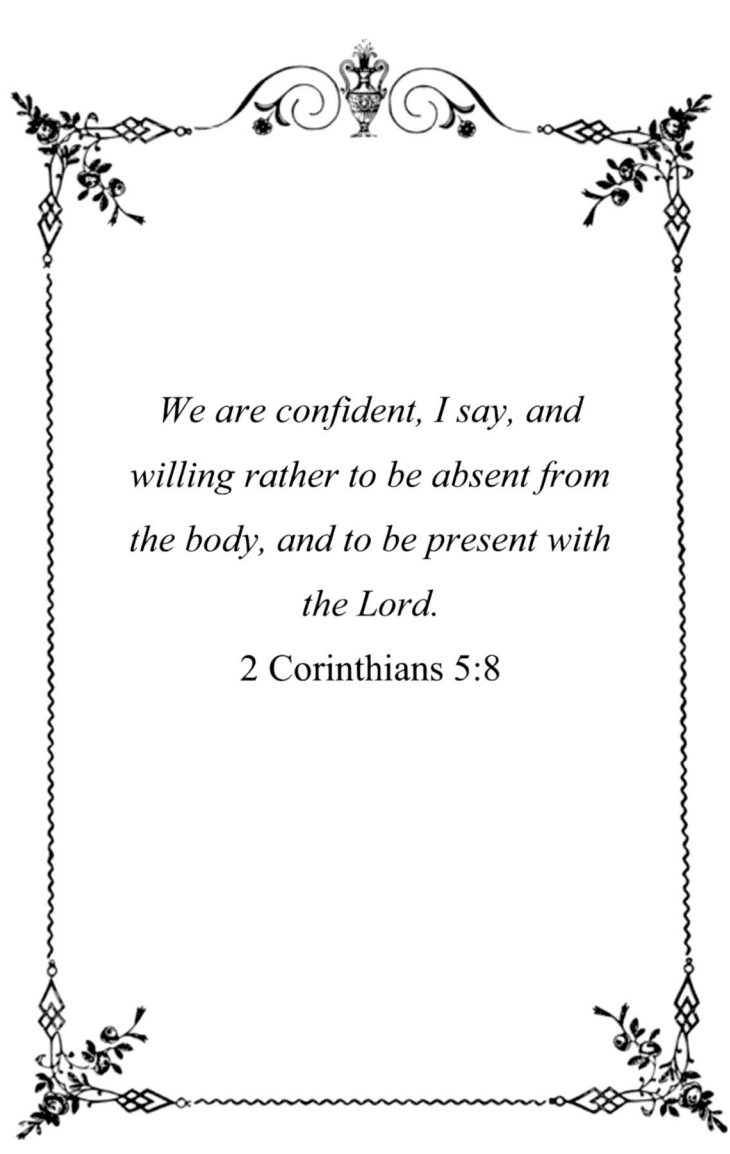

We are confident, I say, and willing rather to be absent from the body, and to be present with the Lord.

2 Corinthians 5:8

Chapter Ten

Caregiving Advice (Personal and Professional)

The world of caregiving, personal or professional cannot be taken frivolously. The art of caregiving is serious business; not to be entered into lightly. It's literally a commitment until death do you part! Accepting the full responsibility of the role, strips you of self and changes your life forever. This is your first revelation; your world becomes second nature to the duty of caregiving. It is a 24-hour, 7-day a week commitment. This is where duty calls, and the honor to use my professional knowledge to manage the events of any given day or night are called upon. Not every facet of caregiving leaves you with a feeling of accomplishment and fulfillment. Sometimes in your humanness you may miss the mark. It is during those times reaching out to family, friends, and professionals becomes your saving grace. By sharing the art of the caregiving, it my earnest desire to help someone (*personally and professionally*) who may find themselves in my shoes. In hindsight, I wish I had given myself permission to feel and act the way I honestly felt without apology when

I did not want to be a caregiver. I realize now, I should have walked…no run away to regroup as mommy's health and my duties became more challenging. Let me share a few words of advice as the daughter, nurse, mother to my mother, and child of the decedent. I am hopeful my encouragement will offer insight into the lived-experiences with caregiving candor. Time, touch, and temperament were key elements of my caregiving experience. Each can be applied to the personal and professional world whenever you find yourself with the awesome responsibly of someone's existence is in your hand.

Time is essential to the caregiving experience. The family member or patient (*based on the location of caregiving)* care cannot be hurried but managed in such a way that the one receiving the care experiences compassionate care. We all have heard the saying, "time waits on no man." In caregiving situations, time awareness is essential to the one under your care. Appointment times, meal times, bath time, medication times and bedtime were centered around mommy. Being productive and using the hours in the day wisely keeps you from feeling consumed with the role of caregiver. This thought is beneficial in the professional practice setting. With four or five patients on a busy hospital unit, demands that you develop good time management skills to get things accomplished every single day. Since time is such a valuable commodity, to the *give*r and to the *receiver*, removing strict time frames from the equation made the art of caregiving less stressful. When I stopped making strict schedules based on how I wanted the day to go, life as a caregiver turned out to be smoother and less stressful. My movements were based on the needs of mommy and not on the needs of me.

Touch as a caregiver is as important as the time you spend giving care. As mommy's health declined and her inability to do for herself, I would do for her like I would want done for me. I must share the story with you about a day when I was brushing her hair. I tell this story because when I brush my hair, ***I brush my hair***. I like firm brushes and I press hard. I brush many times over, back and forth. I was scratching my scalp and brushing my hair at the same time. This touch did not fare well with mommy. I never knew she was tender-headed until I had to brush her hair. *"Ouch, Oooo, that hurts"* she said. Well, I brush my hair this way all the time. It never hurts me, I replied. Did you catch it? *It never hurt me.* The touch and feeling of satisfaction of brushing my hair was not a welcomed encounter for mommy. It hurt! This is one example of the importance of understanding how the laying on of the hands (our nursing oath) is so vital to those we care about and for. It is important to ask how the loved one carried out their daily habits before they could not care for themselves. Daily, it is necessary to put yourself in the place of someone incapable of self-care. Always demonstrate respect, respect their privacy, and reverence the role of caregiving. As a caregiver, you become up close and personal with your loved one and making someone feel comfortable is essential.

Monitoring your temperament requires constant awareness and acknowledgement when you are in a caregiver role. Without keeping temperament in view, one challenging event will sabotage the entire day. Your mood as caregiver that begins your *tour of duty* can often determine the flow of the day. Many artists have written songs that suggest we have good days and bad days as people. On those bad days, hills and valleys can be consuming and compromise our ability to give focused care to our loved one. In all honesty, there are many of those days in the world of giving care, but not in the world of caregiving. Frankly, I wanted no part of the role. When those emotions appeared, I would go to bed saying tomorrow, I'll do better. I would be restored with God's help. I would realize the important role of meals, baths, laundry, brushing hair, preparing medication containers, ordering medical supplies and more. In a professional setting, many of the same realities are front and center. As the caregiver of another, the core and fundamental focus is to acknowledge how you feel and when you feel overwhelmed, overloaded, weary and alone. I wish I would have done this more. There were willing-workers near and far, and I did not take advantage of my help like I should have. I know I upset my family and friends at times, and for that I'm sorry. Don't let your temperament determine your expectations of others. Ask for help! It is ok. Step away! It's ok. The biggest lesson here is…never assume anything as a caregiver (personally or professionally). All of these things are essential when you are in survival mode experiencing the many facets of the lived-experiences surrounding the art of caregiving.

Photo Credit: Eternal Rest Funeral Home, Houston, Texas

Favorite Sayings of Mommy

"What do you do with spilled milk? Clean it up, of course."

Verily, verily, I say unto you, He that believeth on me hath everlasting life.

John 6:47

May the Lord watch, between me and thee, while we are absent, one from another, Amen.

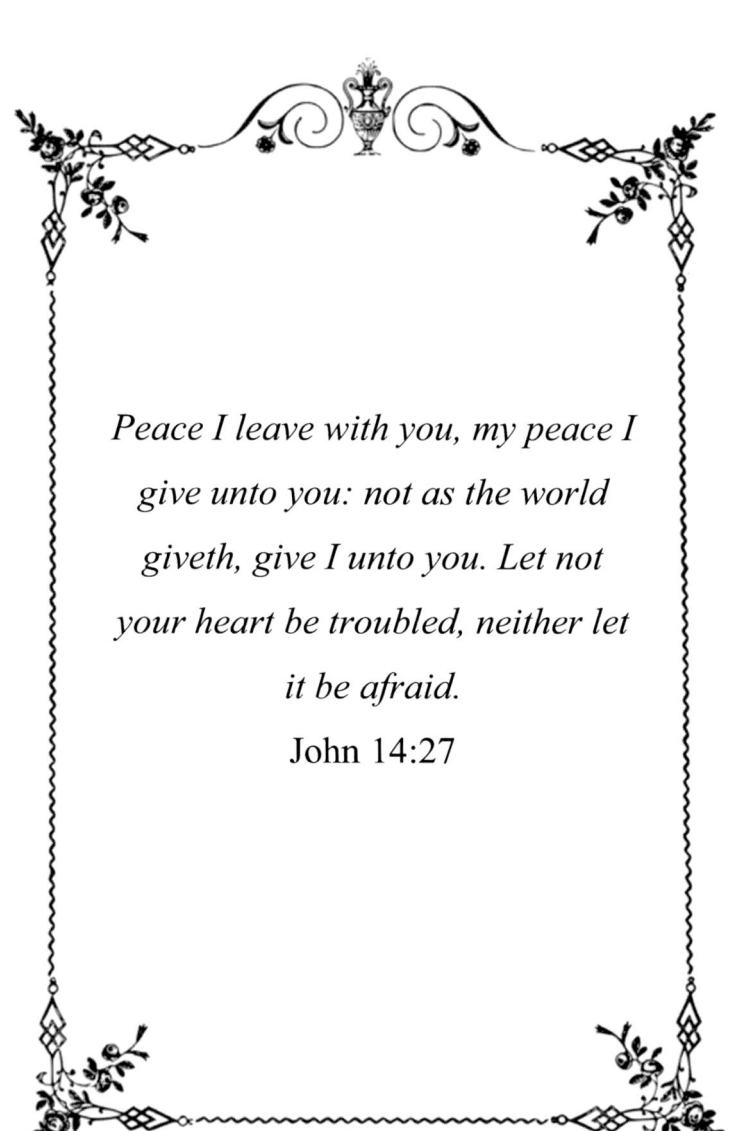

Peace I leave with you, my peace I give unto you: not as the world giveth, give I unto you. Let not your heart be troubled, neither let it be afraid.

John 14:27

See you later Mommy!

About the Author

Dr. Cynthia Jean Hickman completed her Ph.D. in Health Services with a specialization in leadership from Walden University. Her research focus addressed the influences of nutritional food label understanding on African-American Women with obesity. Dr. Hickman obtained her Masters in Nursing with a specialization in nursing education from Walden University, her Bachelors of Science in Nursing from Prairie View A & M University and received a diploma in nursing from the Toledo Hospital School of Nursing, Toledo, Ohio. She has over 30 years of nursing experience in an acute-care setting. Dr. Hickman has written and contributed to academic and non-academic journals. She is an RN to BSN nursing professor at Capella University. Dr. Hickman is the 2019 Social Change Fellow and grant recipient of Walden University. Her research focuses on older adults and family members who serve as their caregivers.

Nursing, leadership, and nutritional health are major passions. With a background that spans the fields of nursing, leadership, education, nutrition and public health, her interest and goals include advancing social change in an individual, community, and global stage.

Made in the USA
Middletown, DE
05 June 2021

40992099R00055